BIG TRUTH L

WHAT THE BIBLE SAYS ABOUT RETIREMENT

Derek Brown

Cliff McManis

With All Wisdom Publications
Cupertino, California

WHAT THE BIBLE SAYS ABOUT RETIREMENT

What the Bible Says About Retirement
Copyright © 2022 Derek Brown & Cliff McManis
Published by WITH ALL WISDOM PUBLICATIONS

Requests for information about **BIG TRUTH** LITTLE BOOKS® can be sent to:

editor@withallwisdom.org

All rights reserved.

ISBN: 978-1-952221-09-5

All Scripture quotations unless otherwise noted are from the: *New American Standard Bible*. Copyright © 1960, 1962, 1963, 1968, 1971, 1972, 1973, 1975, 1977, 1995, 2020 by the Lockman Foundation; the *ESV ® Bible (The Holy Bible, English Standard Version ®)*, Copyright © 2001 by Crossway, a publishing ministry of Good News Publishers; and the *NET Bible (The New English Translation)*, copyright 1996, 2019 by Biblical Studies Press, L.L.C. Used by permission. All rights reserved.

What the Bible Says About Retirement is volume 18 in the **BIG TRUTH** LITTLE BOOKS® series.

Editor-in-Chief: Cliff McManis
General Editor: Derek Brown
Managing Editor: Breanna Paniagua
Cover Design: Oluwasanya Awe
Proofreaders: Tim Anderson, Albert Chen, Gary Leith, John Platz

This work is a publication of WITH ALL WISDOM PUBLICATIONS. No part of this publication may be reproduced, stored in a retrieval system, or transmitted in any form or by any means except by permission of the publisher.

"The righteous person will flourish like the palm tree,
He will grow like a cedar in Lebanon.
Planted in the house of the Lord,
They will flourish in the courtyards of our God.
They will still yield fruit in advanced age;
They will be full of sap and very green"
(Ps 92:12-14)

"And even when I am old and gray,
O God, do not forsake me,
Until I declare Your strength to this generation,
Your power to all who are to come."
(Ps 71:18)

Contents

	Series Preface	ix
1	Retirement: The American Dream?	1
2	How Did We Get Here?	7
3	Retirement and a Theology of Work	13
4	Retirement and a Theology of Wealth	27
5	Storing Up for the Future	41
6	How to Spend Your Retirement Well	51
7	Do Not Grow Weary in Doing Good	59
8	True Retirement	73
9	Conclusion	83

SERIES PREFACE

Our mission with the *BIG TRUTH little books*® series is to provide edifying, accessible literature for Christian readers from all walks of life. We understand that it is often difficult to find time to read good books. But we also understand that reading is a valuable means of spiritual growth. The answer? Get some really big truth into some little books. These books may be small, but each is full of Scripture, theological reflection, and pastoral insight. Our hope is that Christians young and old will benefit from these books as they grow in their knowledge of Christ through His Word.

Cliff McManis, General Editor
Derek Brown, Series Editor

1

RETIREMENT: THE AMERICAN DREAM?

Christian, are you looking forward to your retirement? Are you dreaming of the day when you can close the office door for the last time and enter a new phase of life without the day-to-day weight of work? Are you counting the days until your last child is out of the house so you can get some rest, slow your pace of life, catch up on your favorite hobbies, and pursue some long-awaited travel? Are you anticipating a good one to two decades of unfettered relaxation and recreation?

If so, you are not unlike many Americans who view retirement as the default status for those in their early- to mid-sixties. Culturally, it is simply assumed that the natural course of life is to work for about forty years and begin to taper off around age sixty-five. For many, it seems that the expectation is to spend those last fifteen to twenty years of life in relative ease and recreation. In other words, you work really hard for about four decades in order to enjoy well-earned rest and relaxation and some time to do the things you really want to do in the last two.

Retirement: The Never-Ending Weekend?

In case you think the above description is a mere caricature of how Americans generally view their latter-years, consider how retirement is described at the popular level. One article begins by describing retirement like this: "Ah, retirement. It's the never-ending weekend, that well-deserved oasis of freedom and rest we reach after decades of hard work."[1] An article in U. S. News and World Report encourages readers to "Turn Early Retirement into a Never-Ending Vacation."[2] Another website tells retirees to indulge in some well-deserved "me time" during their retirement.[3]

---

[1] Cella Wright, "Think Retirement is Smooth Sailing? A Look at its Potential Effects on the Brain," at Ideas.Ted.com, July 2, 2019. https://ideas.ted.com/think-retirement-is-smooth-sailing-a-look-at-its-potential-effects-on-the-brain/.

[2] Kathleen Peddicord, "Turn Early Retirement into a Never-Ending Vacation: How Perpetual Travel Became One Couple's New Retirement Lifestyle," at U. S. News and World Report, May 24, 2017, accessed on November 3, 2022, https://money.usnews.com/money/blogs/on-retirement/articles/2017-05-24/turn-early-retirement-into-a-never-ending-vacation.

[3] "The Art of Good Living: 10 Tips to Enjoy a Happy Retirement Life," at Our Father's House and Soup Kitchen," June 27, 2021, accessed on November 3, 2022, https://ofhsoupkitchen.org/happy-retirement-life.

One doesn't have to search long to find a seemingly never-ending array of lifestyle blogs, online magazines, and financial institutions that provide resources aimed specifically help people plan for and spend their retirement.[4]

The truth is that retirement is a ubiquitous reality in our modern American experience, and something we are conditioned to think about often. Consider how compensation packages are structured. One of the standard benefits that companies will offer potential employees is a retirement plan like a 401(k). This means that at your very first job out of college you are already preparing for when you will no longer be working.

But even if you didn't receive a 401(k) in your most recent compensation package, you live in a country where retirement is the default status for those between the ages of sixty-two to sixty-seven.[5] From a federal government perspective, Social Security is designed to help you ease into your latter years when you won't be

---

[4] See, for example, "Retirement Income: Spending Your Savings," at https://investor.vanguard.com/investor-resources-education/retirement/income; Kathleen Coxwell, "120 Big Ideas for What to Do in Retirement," at NewRetirement.com, June 24, 2021, accessed November 3, 2022, https://www.newretirement.com/retirement/what-to-do-in-retirement/; Rita Call, "What to do in Retirement: 20 Serious (and Fun!) Things to Keep You Busy! At SixtyAndMe.com, July 7, 2022, accessed on November 3, 2022, https://sixtyandme.com/20-serious-and-fun-things-you-can-do-in-retirement/.

[5] Julia Kagan, "Retirement" at Investopedia, November 19, 2019, Updated July 16, 2021 https://www.investopedia.com/terms/r/retirement.asp. This statistic is based on a survey conducted by the U. S. Census Bureau.

earning an income by providing you with a guaranteed monthly check. No longer burdened with the need to put in a forty-to-fifty-hour work week to secure an income, retirees launch out into a new stage of life with more time and flexibility, often viewing their retirement through the lens of vacation. "Today," Jeff Haanen, Founder and Executive Director of Denver Institute for Faith and Work, writes, "the dominant paradigm of retirement is about vacation—how to afford it, and then how to make the most of it."[6]

Retire Early?
But retirement is no longer only for those who are in their early to mid sixties. A movement among a younger generation is gaining traction, known by the acronym, F.I.R.E.—Financial Independence Retire Early. The goal among F.I.R.E. advocates is to "save enough money to give them the freedom they want and avoid depending on a regular job to pay the bills."[7] F.I.R.E. practitioners will take measures—sometimes severe— to limit their expenses so they can increase their month-to-month savings. Through the combination of careful investing and aggressive savings, F.I.R.E. proponents labor to amass enough money so that they will no longer be tethered to their regular job and therefore have the

---

[6] Jeff Haanen, *An Uncommon Guide to Retirement* (Chicago: Moody, 2019), 20.
[7] Kelly Anne Smith, "How to Retire Early with FIRE," at Forbes.com, December 20, 2021, https://www.forbes.com/advisor/retirement/the-forbes-guide-to-fire/.

freedom to pursue other interests that better fit their "passions," whether it's travel or starting a business.[8]

Retirement in this sense doesn't always mean that the retirees have stopped working completely, but only that they have placed themselves in a financial position where they are no longer beholden to obligations set by their manager. The aim is generally the same as a traditional retiree, however. In both cases, each group looks forward to the freedom to do what they most want to do instead of remaining under the supervision of an employer. Autonomy is the aim.

The point of this brief survey is to simply observe that the concept of retirement is pervasive throughout our society. We begin our working life with an aim toward retirement, we spend a good portion of our career laboring to fund it, and we daydream about how we will spend it. Some of us are even trying to enter the retirement phase decades before our sixties.

The question that Christians need to answer is, "How does our Lord want us to think about retirement?" Answering this question is the primary aim of this book. We want to help believers in the Lord Jesus rightly assess the contemporary view of retirement in light of Scripture and then apply what we find in

---

[8] "Is Financial Independence Possible? At Fidelity.com, August 23, 2022, https://www.fidelity.com/learning-center/personal-finance/financial-independence-retire-early-FIRE.
Kelly Anne Smith, "How to Retire Early with FIRE."

God's Word to our own approach to work and retirement.

But before we start our assessment, we must ask a few more foundational questions, such as, "How did we get here? How did the concept of retirement develop within our American society?" That is the topic of our next chapter.

2

HOW DID WE GET HERE?

Catalysts of Change

In the previous chapter, we considered how Americans generally view retirement. By a brief survey of popular articles and common definitions, we determined that Americans, by and large, view their retirement as a time when they can finally stop working and enjoy some well-earned rest and relaxation. For those who have been able to save enough or accrue enough Social Security benefits, this phase of life usually begins in one's early to mid sixties. The question we want to ask in this chapter is, how did this view toward retirement develop? Has it always been this way? What sociological, economic, and medical changes have occurred in this country's history that have shaped our view of retirement?

According to research conducted by the Georgetown University Law School, we should start our timeline in America at 1875, when the American Express company created the first pension plan.[9] At this point in our nation's history, about seventy-five percent of all males over the age of sixty-five were working. If they were not working, it was likely due to a disability that physically kept them out of the workforce. By 1900, life expectancy was forty-nine years old, and those who lived to age sixty could expect to live, on average, another twelve years. Nevertheless, most workers continued to labor as long as they were physically able.

Between 1900 and 1918, private pension plans continued to grow, until 1919, when over 300 pension plans served about fifteen percent of the workforce. These pension plans had a clear purpose. "The growth in pension coverage is attributed to employers' desire to attract workers, reduce labor turnover," and "more [humanely] remove older, less productive employees."

In 1935, Social Security was enacted which established sixty-five as the standard retirement age. The government set the retirement age at sixty-five by following the practice of pension programs that were already in place and the federal Railroad Retirement System passed a year earlier.[10] Even so, when Social

---

[9] "A Timeline of the Evolution of Retirement in the United States," https://scholarship.law.georgetown.edu/cgi/viewcontent.cgi?article=1049&context=legal.
[10] "Age 65 Retirement: The German Precedent," SocialSecurity.gov, https://www.ssa.gov/history/age65.html.

Security was enacted, it was "believed most workers will not live for an extended period after retirement and thus will receive Social Security benefits for a minimal amount of time."[11] By 1940, around 4.1 million private-sector workers (fifteen percent of all private-sector workers) would be covered by a pension plan. Like Social Security, these plans were designed to protect people from poverty in their old age. Yet, also like Social Security, these pension plans were expected to pay out benefits for only a short period after retirement. By 1945, with nearly seventy-five percent of Americans paying income tax, tax-deferred savings programs like pensions became increasingly attractive.

Just over thirty years later, the Revenue Act of 1978 established Code Section 401(k) plans which allowed employees to set aside some of their pre-tax income each pay period in a tax-deferred account that could be later withdrawn in retirement. In 1984, the Retirement Equity Act (REA) was enacted. The REA allowed employees to start saving for retirement earlier by lowering the minimum age that a plan may require for enrollment from age twenty-five to age twenty-one, while also lowering the minimum age for vesting service from age twenty-two to age eighteen.[12] By 2006, life

---

[11] A Timeline of the Evolution of Retirement in the United States," https://scholarship.law.georgetown.edu/cgi/viewcontent.cgi?article=1049&context=legal.

[12] Vesting refers to an employee's ownership of his retirement account. Some business require an employee to work a certain amount of time in

expectancy was seventy-four for men and seventy-nine for women. Someone who reaches the age of sixty-five can expect to live longer; until eighty-one for a man and eighty-four for a woman.

Lessons Learned

We believe there is a confluence of at least three factors in America that have led to our current view of retirement: (1) A strong and vibrant economy has given Americans access to a significant and historically unprecedented amount of wealth.[13] (2) Such wealth has created the opportunity for the intentional development of government-based and privately-funded retirement plans to provide for workers and spouses in their old age.[14] (3) Longer life-expectancies now make it possible to plan for a time in your life when you can have a steady income without a job and no need to work (due to

---

order to vest full ownership of their account through "graded" or "cliff" vesting. In the former, ownership increases incrementally over a period set by the employer. In the latter, the employee receives complete ownership of his retirement account immediately upon completing a required period of employment. Some companies do not require a vesting period and grant full ownership of employee's retirement account upon their employment.

[13] See Alan Greenspan and Adrian Wooldridge, *Capitalism in America: A History* (New York: Penguin Press, 2018).

[14] One article estimates that there is more than $4.8 trillion currently in 401(k) assets. See Kathleen Elkins, "A brief history of the 401(k), which changed how Americans retire," at CNBC, January 4, 2017, https://www.cnbc.com/2017/01/04/a-brief-history-of-the-401k-which-changed-how-americans-retire.html. That's 1 trillion more than Germany's entire GDP.

factors 1-2), *and* several extra years to enjoy your non-working life.

Economically, many Americans can create enough wealth so that they don't have to work as much or at all in their later years. Medically, we are living longer and with better healthcare which means we have more time with which to spend our retirement years. This has led to the development of a social ideal that retirement is a time when you stop working to spend a good bulk of your time on recreational pursuits and to enjoy a season of well-deserved rest.

But even before we assess the legitimacy of such a view of retirement, our assumption in this book is that many Christians have been influenced, in some measure, by this view of retirement. From our combined experience in pastoral ministry over several decades, we have noticed a lack of sharp distinction between unbelievers and believers on this issue of retirement. Many Christians seem to assume that the normal state for someone in their early to mid sixties is to stop working and take some extended time off until they die and go to heaven. Our prayer is that this book will help you develop a more biblically robust—and, as it turns out, more satisfying—view of work and retirement.

But, in order to talk about retirement *from* work, we need to first develop a biblical theology *of* work and a biblical theology of money. We will address the topic of work in our next chapter.

3

RETIREMENT AND A THEOLOGY OF WORK

God is the Original Worker

From the very first page of the Bible, we see that that God is the Master Worker. He is the designer, builder, and craftsman of all things. Over the course of six days, God fashioned a massive universe in which to place an inhabitable planet. In this planet he designed an assortment of animals and insects, along with a variety of fauna and flora. The sun and moon were placed in the sky for the sake of his image-bearers (see Gen 1:1-24).

When God created humankind in his own image, he made the man and the woman workers. Their work was to exercise dominion over the earth, to subdue it, to bring it under their rulership and make it useful to themselves and others (Gen 1:26-31). In Genesis 2, God zooms in on what happened on the sixth day. He created Adam, breathed into his nostrils the breath of life and immediately placed him into the garden to "work it and keep it" (Gen 2:15).

Work is Good

It is important to keep in mind that God gave Adam the assignment to work and keep the garden *prior* to the Fall. Therefore, our capacity for productive labor and our call to exercise dominion over the creation is a fundamental aspect of our personhood. Work is not a necessary evil that God laid upon our shoulders after the Fall; it is a gift that God provided his image-bearers prior to the entrance of sin into the world. (We will return to the truth that God designed us specifically to work when we address recent studies which indicate that full-blown retirement may not be good for your health.)

It isn't until after the Fall and the curse that the woman and the man found their work to be frustrating and painful. Their work was still good, but now due to the curse, their work was often beset with difficulty and regular futility (Gen 3:16-19).

Nevertheless, as we move on from Genesis, we learn that God still places a high premium on our calling to exercise dominion and engage in productive labor. This emphasis on productive labor became foundational later in Israel's economy when God established them as a nation in the days of Moses. Basic to their economy was a six-day work week. God instructed Israel to work six days out of the week, and to rest on the seventh (Exod 23:12). Six out of the seven days of the week, the Israelites were to be engaged in productive labor to provide for themselves, their families, and the benefit of the greater community. One day out of the week was designated for worship and rest from daily labor.

Expectedly, Israel's wisdom literature contains a significant amount of practical instruction on the topic of work, as Solomon often links diligence with wisdom and laziness with folly. Unwillingness to work usually leads to poverty, but diligence leads to abundance. "The sluggard does not plow in the autumn;" Solomon observes, "he will seek at harvest and have nothing" (Prov 20:4). "The plans of the diligent," he says a few verses later, "lead surely to abundance, but everyone who is hasty comes only to poverty" (Prov 21:5).

Solomon even exhorts his readers to learn from the ant and cultivate a life of proactive labor: "Go to the ant, O sluggard; consider her ways, and be wise. Without having any chief, officer, or ruler, she prepares her bread in summer and gathers her food in harvest" (Prov 6:6-8). These observations are grounded in creation realities established in Genesis 1-2: God has designed humankind to use their God-given abilities to create, provide for themselves, exercise dominion, and engage in productive labor for the benefit of fellow image-bearers. To neglect this calling is to live contrary to the way God has designed the world to function, which is the very definition of foolishness (see Prov 24:30-34).

The New Testament Ethic

The New Testament affirms the high value of work that God established in the Old Testament. Jesus, for example, instructs his disciples to multiply their talents. A "talent" in Jesus' day was a large sum of money. In the parable, the talents represent the resources that Christ has given his disciples: financial assets, spiritual gifts, time, energy, opportunities, and natural talents. Jesus' disciples are to make good use of these resources for the glory of God and the furtherance of his kingdom and not hide them in the ground. Indeed, the two servants who multiplied their master's money were commended. The servant who hid his master's money in the ground was chastised for his laziness (Matt 25:14-30).

In his letter to the Ephesians, Paul says to the new convert, "Let the thief no longer steal, but rather let him labor, doing honest work with his own hands, so that he may have something to share with anyone in need" (Eph 4:28). In 1 Thessalonians 4:11-12, Paul instructs the believers to "aspire to live quietly, and to mind your own affairs, and to work with your hands, as we instructed you, so that you may walk properly before outsiders and be dependent on no one." Interestingly, the word for "aspire" is the same word that Paul uses when he says, "I make it my *ambition* to preach the gospel, not where Christ has already been named" (Rom 15:20) and when he says in 2 Cor 5:9 that he always makes it his aim to please the Lord. In other words, it is a worthy, God-pleasing thing to live quietly, work, earn your own living, and not be dependent on anyone. In his second letter to the Thessalonians, Paul admonished some people in the congregation for not working.

> [6]Now we command you, brothers, in the name of our Lord Jesus Christ, that you keep away from any brother who is walking in idleness and not in accord with the tradition that you received from us. [7]For you yourselves know how you ought to imitate us, because we were not idle when we were with you, [8]nor did we eat anyone's bread without paying for it, but with toil and labor we worked night and day, that we might not be a burden to any of you. [9]It was not because we do not have that right, but to give you in ourselves an example to imitate. [10]For even when we were with you, we would give you this command: If anyone is not willing to work, let him not eat. [11]For we hear that some among you walk in idleness, not busy at work, but busybodies. [12]Now such persons we command and encourage in the

Lord Jesus Christ to do their work quietly and to earn their own living (2 Thess 3:6-12).

According to Paul, so important was it to work, that a person's unwillingness to engage in productive labor would earn them the rebuke of the congregation and disqualify them from receiving food. Paul even engaged in useful work to relieve the Thessalonians' obligation to provide for him. Due to his status as an apostle, Paul could have received material support from the believers in Thessalonica (cf. 1 Cor 9:6-13). But in order to provide a godly example to the members of the church, Paul declined his right to receive financial provision from these believers and chose rather to support himself.

So concerned was he about professing Christians engaging in productive labor that Paul classifies the one who doesn't work and provide for his household as "worse than an unbeliever" (1 Tim 5:8). Young widows are instructed to remarry soon, bear children, and work diligently in the home (1 Tim 5:14) so that they don't open themselves up to accusation for being an unproductive, idle busybody (1 Tim 5:13). Indeed, only widows who reached a certain age threshold (sixty years of age or older) would qualify for financial assistance from the church *if* they had a reputation of godly diligence prior to the death of their husband (1 Tim 5:9-10). The expectation is that such a widow would be just as diligent in her later years as she was previously.

We have taken this brief tour through Scripture to lay a biblical view of work alongside our modern-day, American conception of retirement which compels us to look forward to a time in our lives when we no longer have to work. On the whole, Scripture highly values work, considers it a vital component of our human personhood and calling as God's image-bearers, and admonishes those who refuse to work. So, it doesn't seem that retirement, as it is understood by many in America as a time when you stop working and focus on recreational pursuits and hobbies, is a biblical category.

Legitimate Transitions
Nevertheless, for many people working today, it may be unwise for them to continue in their current line of work into old age. For example, people working in construction, operating heavy-equipment, or laboring in some other kind of physically demanding job simply can't work at the same intensity or in the same way into their old age. Retirement from this type of physically demanding labor is often necessary for the sake of the employee's health and safety. There are also cases when a person may be forced into retirement because of an injury.

So, we are certainly not suggesting that the concept of retirement is inherently sinful. Even the Levitical priests were allowed to hold their post only until age fifty (Num 8:25). So, the priests of the Tabernacle were forced into retirement by God at a certain season in life.

This restriction may have been due to the fact that maintaining the sacrificial system was, physically speaking, a highly demanding job. In their case, God created an age restriction on the priests for their own protection.

Therefore, we can acknowledge each of the above contemporary circumstances where retirement from a *particular kind of work* due to age or injury is entirely legitimate, while also saying that Scripture does not have us looking forward to a time in our lives when we *stop working*. Even if we can quit our current job and no longer need regular income because of a retirement account, pension, or Social Security, we are exhorted throughout the New Testament to engage in good works. God saved us for the express purpose of good works (Eph 2:10). The people of God should be known as those who are zealous for good works (Titus 2:14) and devoted to maintaining consistent fruitfulness (Titus 3:14). Good works should characterize the life of the Christian, regardless of our age (Matt 5:14-16; 1 Tim 6:17-19). These good works include faithfulness at a job (Eph 6:8) and serving and blessing others outside of our place of employment.

In other words, Scripture doesn't encourage us to look forward to a time when we are relieved of serving the Lord and serving others through productive labor. As we age, our productive labor and good works will take a different shape because we are getting older and don't have the same strength and energy as we used to.

The Bible is realistic about the aging process. Paul reminds us that with time "our physical body is wearing away" (2 Cor 4:16). The process of physical death is not pleasant, and its unpleasantness needs to be acknowledged. In Ecclesiastes, Solomon detailed in unparalleled poetic description the process of physical decline, from head to toe, when he described the pains of getting older. He himself was an aged, declining old man who had lost all his youthful strength:

> Remember also your Creator in the days of your youth, before the evil days come and the years approach when you will say, "I have no pleasure in them"; before the sun and the light, the moon and the stars are darkened, and clouds return after the rain; on the day that the watchmen of the house tremble, and strong men are bent over, the grinders stop working because they are few, and those who look through windows grow dim; and the doors on the street are shut as the sound of the grinding mill is low, and one will arise at the sound of the bird, and all the daughters of song will sing softly. Furthermore, *people* are afraid of a high place and of terrors on the road; the almond tree blossoms, the grasshopper drags itself along, and the caper berry is ineffective. For man goes to his eternal home while the mourners move around in the street. *Remember*

your Creator before the silver cord is broken and the golden bowl is crushed, the pitcher by the spring is shattered and the wheel at the cistern is crushed; then the dust will return to the earth as it was, and the spirit will return to God who gave it (Eccl 12:1-7).

But despite the challenges and vulnerabilities that come with physical aging, the Bible also speaks of the unique abilities that come from growing older, like the experience and wisdom that accompanies it, energized by the Spirit of God. For Paul reminds us that even though our physical body is decaying daily, God is renewing our "inner man day by day" after the image of Christ (2 Cor 4:16; cf. Rom 8:29). And for the Christian, God uses the sanctified experience and wisdom of the elderly to edify and bless his Church in unique ways. Older believers have an arsenal of unique, time-tested, rare, intangible gifts with which to bless the Body of Christ including practical wisdom, availability, flexibility with time, a long-term perspective, Spirit-guided patience, tempered sensibilities, tenderized convictions, an imminent sense of the brevity of life, and much more.

The twilight years are a new opportunity of service to God for prospective retirees. The calling to make the most of our time, maximize our gifts and talents, serve the Lord, and engage in productive labor that makes us useful to others doesn't stop at age sixty-five.

Interestingly, there are developments within our contemporary society that affirm this biblical outlook on work and retirement. In light of what we've discussed about how God has designed and purposed us to be workers, we shouldn't be surprised by recent studies which suggest that retirement, when it is approached as a time when we don't work and just take the next fifteen years off, is not good for our health. Consider these recent findings:

- Formal retirement can raise one's risk of succumbing to various physical ailments such as "severe cardiovascular disease and cancer…[and] increased risk factors (e.g., BMI, cholesterol, blood pressure) and increased problems in physical activities."[15]
- Another study conducted by the *Journal of Health Economics* suggests that retirees may experience a cognitive decline in their post-work years that would be offset by continued labor.[16]
- Richard Johnson at the *Wall Street Journal* examined evidence that suggested that setting aside the daily routine of work can

---

[15] Stephanie Behncke, "Does Retirement Trigger Ill Health," in *Journal of Health Economics.*, March 2012: 282-300. Accessed October 1, 2020.
[16] Eric Bonsang, Stephane Adam, Sergio Perelman, "Does Retirement Affect Cognitive Functioning?" in *Journal of Health Economics*, March 2012: 490-501. Accessed October 1, 2020.

lead to the development of more sedentary and otherwise unhealthy habits like increased eating, drinking, and smoking.[17]
- The lack of purposeful work can also result in a kind of aimlessness and depression.[18]

Given what we know about our design by God to exercise dominion, work, and engage in productive labor, the findings of these scientific studies and broader societal developments make sense: our minds and bodies were not designed by God to disengage from productive labor in service of God and others. Inasmuch as we are physically and mentally capable, we are to keep laboring for the good of others. Yes, the nature and intensity of our work will likely change as we get older, but our aim as Christians should always be to bless others through useful work.

Because of our current cultural setting, it is likely that many Christians reading this book will need to readjust their thinking on retirement to better reflect biblical values and priorities. Our hope for you is that if you do find that your expectations about retirement have been

---

[17] Richard W. Johnson, "The Case Against Early Retirement," in *The Wall Street Journal*, April 21, 2019. Accessed October 1, 2020.

[18] Marguerite Ward, "4 Science-Backed Ways to Cope with Depression When You've Lost Your Job and Feel Like You Also Lost Your Sense of Purpose," in Business Insider, October 9, 2020, https://www.businessinsider.com/how-to-deal-with-unemployment-depression-depressed-psychologist. Accessed January 28, 2022.

shaped more by the prevailing culture than God's Word, you will give serious thought and prayer to what Scripture teaches and ask God to help you make the most of your latter years for his glory.

4

Retirement and a Theology of Wealth

When talking about retirement we inevitably must talk about money and wealth. The Bible talks about money, wealth, and possessions from beginning to end, a total of about 1,800 times, from Genesis (12:5; 13:2) to Revelation (18:3). Scripture is the authority on the topic of money. God ordained the principles of economics, the exchange of valuables, commodities, and services, from the very beginning of creation to foster social interaction between people. The reality of currency comes directly from God. The exchange of wealth for goods and services is not a by-product of social evolution, nor is it an artificial convention invented by humans. God is the ultimate authority on money and wealth because he is the Creator and has laid out all the laws and structures in the world by which humanity would live and conduct their lives (Eccl 3:1-11). And God has communicated everything he wants us to know about money and wealth in his Word, the Bible. For every topic we confront in this life, God's Word is sufficient to tell us everything we need to know about how to live a life pleasing to the Lord (2 Pet 1:3).

Many folks have a wrong-headed view of retirement because they have a wrong view of money. It is very easy for believers to be influenced by the thinking of the world (1 Cor 15:33), to imbibe its worldviews, to assimilate secular thinking in many areas of life—often unwittingly. When Christians do absorb worldly thinking they are then thrown off-kilter in daily living and actually live in conflict with God's will and desires. So, to further lay a solid foundation by which to think about retirement, let's consider some basic biblical principles about money.

God Owns Everything

The first verse in the Bible declares, "In the beginning God created the heavens and the earth" (Gen 1:1). God is the Creator and as such he owns everything. He is the "possessor of heaven and earth" (Gen 14:22). Scripture further proclaims that "everything in heaven and earth" is God's (1 Chron 29:11). God himself reminds us in Psalms when he says, "every beast of the forest is Mine, the cattle on a thousand hills" (50:10); and in Isaiah he asserts, "Heaven is My throne and the earth is My footstool" (66:1). Because he is the Creator, every person that ever existed belongs to God: "Behold all souls are Mine; the soul of the father as well as the soul of the son is Mine" (Ezek 18:4). In keeping with this Paul reminds Christians that not even our body belongs to us: "you are not your own" (1 Cor 6:19). Our bodies belong to God for he created us and he also bought us (1 Cor 6:20) with the blood of Christ (Acts 20:28), the most valuable commodity of all. This truth is utterly foundational in determining how we should think about money, material possessions, valuables, our investments, our retirement plans and our very own lives. God owns it all, from all the cattle on every hill, to our very being, to everything on earth.

Because God owns it all, that means we actually "own" nothing. Whatever we do have is a gift from him. "Every good thing given and every perfect gift is from above, coming down from the Father of lights" (James 1:17). Every valuable thing you and I own came directly from God. Paul reminds every believer in his rhetorical question, "What do you have that you did not receive?" (1 Cor 4:7). What he means is, "Everything you possess, you received from God as a gift." Then he goes on to ask, "And if you did receive it, why do you boast as if you had not received it?" What he means here is, "Some of you Christians actually think you attained valuable and good things in this life by yourself without God's help—how arrogant and wrong you are!" Four times in the discussion Paul calls the Corinthian believers "arrogant" because they forgot about their utter dependence upon God for all things (cf. 1 Cor 4:6, 18, 19, 5:2).

King David knew this truth. He declared to God, "Both riches and honor come from you...Everything comes from you, and we have given you only what comes from your hand...It comes from your hand, and all of it belongs to you" (1 Chron 29:12, 14, 16).

Practically, all this means that even the money we possess belongs to God. We are stewards of God's money. This was true in Moses' day in the Old Testament. God reminded his people that their money was actually his. He declared, "Thus all the tithe of the land, of the seed of the land or the fruit of the tree, is the LORD's" (Lev 27:30).

Money is Not Evil
Today when we think of "money" we think of paper dollar bills and metal coins, and even credit cards. But for most of history money, or better "wealth," did not exist in such fixed, tangible form. Rather, money was in the form of an exchange of values that took place through bartering and trading needed goods with each other. Historically, wealth was also in the form of land or property owned. Printed coins did not arrive on the scene until about the 8th century B.C. So, the word "money" is not limited to "cash" or coinage but includes wealth in all its forms. In the days of Abraham

(c. 2100 BC) there was no form of paper or plastic currency as we have today, but there was money and wealth in the form of tangible possessions of all sorts, from animals, to precious metals, to property, and even to household servants. Abraham even had his own personal standing army of 318 men (Gen 14:14). The Bible says plainly, "Abram was very rich in livestock, in silver, and in gold" (13:2). The Lord made Abraham "rich" giving him "flocks and herds, and silver and gold, and servants and maids, and camels and donkeys" (24:35).

Abraham became rich because God made him reach that status. So, the Bible is clear. Money is not evil. People misquote the Bible routinely saying, "Money is the root of all evil" or by saying, "Money is evil." But that is not God's perspective. God actually said, "the *love* of money is a root of all sorts of evil, and some by longing for it have wandered away from the faith and pierced themselves with many griefs" (1 Tim 6:10; emphasis added). Money is just a tool or mechanism established by God for our good. The human heart is the problem. As fallen humans we misuse and pervert all of God's good gifts. All people are naturally sinful and we easily fall prey to the love or "lust" for money and material possessions. That is what Paul is warning Christians about in this verse. He cautions, "Hey Christian—don't get caught up in the sinful world's thinking about amassing wealth to just spend on your pleasures at retirement when you get older. It may steer you away from being faithful to Christ." Ultimately, money does not satisfy. Our sinful hearts are insatiable. "He who loves money will not be satisfied with money, nor he who loves abundance with its income" (Eccl 5:10). Money is not evil; people are.

God Gives the Power to Make Wealth

Scripture teaches that God is the one who allows people to make money. This is the very thing he said to Moses: "you shall remember the LORD your God, for it is He who is giving you power to make wealth" (Deut 8:18). God is sovereign over every area of our lives. He is in complete control. "[O]ur God is in the heavens; He does whatever He pleases" (Ps 115:3). And when it comes to our personal wealth, God pleases to bless each of us differently. To some people he gives minimal wealth, to some he gives moderately, and to others he gives great wealth. In the parable of the talents (Matt 25:14ff.), a talent referred to wealth or valuable possessions. One servant received five talents, the second two talents, and the last one talent. The Master who owned the talents distributed them out in different increments at his sole discretion. They were not given based on merit or the worth of the individual. It was sheerly a sovereign distribution of the Master. That is what God does. He gives to each person sovereignly as he sees fit.

The Bible does give clues as to the means of God's distribution of wealth to individuals. People attain wealth from God typically in three ways: through hard work, through personal giftedness and through providence. The first way is a principle that applies to virtually anyone as a universal truth. God created us to work and to be productive. If we work diligently, then our work will yield a fruitful by-product. "Poor is the one who works with a lazy hand, but the hand of the diligent makes rich" (Prov 10:4). "The hand of the diligent will rule, but the lazy hand will be put to forced labor" (Prov 12:24).

Some people work very hard their whole life and are yet unable to accumulate wealth exponentially, thus never rising to the level of being in the "upper class." Many faithful, hard-working people live month-to-month or paycheck-to-paycheck their whole lives. But there are those who seem to rise above the fray and grow in wealth and become "wealthy." They don't achieve such status apart from God. God is the one who gives the power to make wealth. God the Creator gives the "wealthy" their money-making ability. This is the second way of attaining wealth: through personal giftedness from God. This gift comes in the form of an aptitude, skill, temperament, providential opportunity, and many other expressions. Some people have a natural, uncanny ability to make money, and lots of it.

The third way God provides wealth is through providence by gifts from others. It may be an inheritance from being born into a wealthy family. It may be a result of marrying into a wealthy family. It may be a result of receiving a gift from a friend or an anonymous donor. This kind of wealth does not come from working hard or even from being gifted at making money. It comes from God's sovereign choice of putting certain people in specific, unique positions to be beneficiaries of tremendous wealth. God is the one who determines before creation when we will be born and where we will be born (Acts 17:26). If we are born into a poor family or born into royalty, that was God's intent for his holy purposes (Eph 1:11).

In addition to the above truths, Jesus also taught that believers need to trust in God the Father as the gracious provider regardless of one's social or economic status. God provides for all of his children. Jesus said, "your Father knows what you need before you ask Him" (Matt 6:8). Therefore, as a child of God, you are not to "be worried about your life, as to what you will eat or what you will drink; nor for your body, as to what you will put on" (v. 25). Your heavenly Father will provide what you need to eat, drink, and clothes to wear (v. 31), "for your heavenly Father knows that you need all these things" (v. 32). God calls believers to be content with their financial status. "For we have brought nothing into the world, so we cannot take anything out of it either. If we have food and covering, with these we shall be content" (1 Tim 6:7-8). Paul promised, "my God will supply all your needs according to His riches in glory in Christ Jesus" (Phil 4:19). King David, at the end of his long life, recounted God's faithful provision for all his children with this amazing testimony: "I have been young and now I am old, Yet I have not seen the righteous forsaken Or his descendants begging bread" (Ps 37:25).

As Christians, we need to remember that God is the one who empowers us to make money and it is his sovereign choice as to what that will look like. Our job is to be thankful and content.

God Has Given Us Clear Priorities for How We Should Handle Money

Many times, if I go into a bank on a Friday to make a transaction, the bank teller will ask, "Aren't you glad it's almost the weekend? Time to unwind and go play," or some kindred sentiment. Or in a similar vein, when shopping at the grocery store, I hear at times the store's loudspeakers playing the song from 1981 called, "Working for the Weekend." That song perfectly sums up the mentality of the world about why we work and make money. They say we make money during the week to go play, and blow that income, on the weekend. It's all about immediate gratification—no long-term, meaningful plans. Or if there is a long-term plan for our money, it is the hollow, self-centered, and relatively recent American version of retirement: save all my money now to go on a permanent vacation from life when I retire at sixty-five. This book is about exposing that false worldview and replacing it with God's perspective.

To that end, we need to be reminded of why God has designed us to work and make money. We need to align our purposes with his. That's all that matters. Scripture is very simple and clear on this issue of why we make money. Or another way to ask the question is, "What does God want me to spend money on?" There are at least four main expectations God has for us as his stewards of our income; he wants us to make money to make a living, to share with others, to give to him and to enjoy life.

We saw in the previous chapter on the theology of work that God expects us to labor diligently to make money so we can pay the bills. This includes earning money to meet all our basic needs: food, clothing, housing, and providing for the immediate family. Previous Scriptures showed us that Paul commanded Christians to derive a self-sustaining income rather than being dependent on others, becoming a burden to them by imposing upon their hard-earned labor. Proverbs 12:11 says, "He who tills his land will have plenty of bread." A responsible husband and father will work as hard as he needs to in order to provide for his family. Also, the godly wife and mother of Proverbs 31 worked hard to help pay the bills and meet the needs of the family: "She looks for wool and flax And works with her hands in delight…She considers a field and buys it; From her earnings she plants a vineyard" (vv. 13, 16).

In addition to paying our bills responsibly, God wants us to make money so we can share it with others.

Giving to others is a basic Christian virtue. Giving reflects God's character and nature. God so loved the world that he "gave" (John 3:16). Jesus commanded his followers to give (Luke 6:38). Sinful human nature is naturally the opposite of God—we are inescapably selfish and stingy. But giving generously to others is a tangible expression of love and a mark of being spiritually born-again. John the Apostle told believers that if they are true Christians then they will be characterized by gracious giving toward other needy believers. And he also said that if you do not give to those in need when you have the means to do so, then you probably don't love God. In other words, you are a phony and not a true child of God (1 John 3:13-18). The early church was marked by godly giving and sharing: "And all the believers were together and had all things in common; and they would sell their property and possessions and share them with all, to the extent that anyone had need" (Acts 2:44-45). Barnabas, a wealthy Christian in Jerusalem, sold some of his property and gave the proceeds to needy people in his church (Acts 4:34-37). God wants us to make money so we can share with those in need.

A third reason God enables us to make money is so we can honor him directly with it. Proverbs 3:9 says, "Honor the LORD from your wealth and from the first of all your produce." "Honor" here is a command and it means "give!" So, the command is to give to God from your wealth. And what we are to give him is the first of our produce or income. That means give to God "off the top," from the first fruits. Every time you receive a paycheck, whether daily, weekly, monthly, or irregularly on commission, the first thing to consider is giving some of that paycheck to God. This is an act of worship. We don't give to God because he needs it. God needs nothing from us. Giving to him is a way of saying "Thank you!" to God the Provider.

In the next verse, Proverbs 3:10, God promised to bless those who obey this command of giving from the first of all of our income. In the Old Testament, during the Old Covenant economy, God's people gave directly to him by giving tithes and sacrifices to the priests. In the New Testament economy, God wants his people to give directly to him by giving to the leaders in the local church. The early saints in the church at Jerusalem gave their money regularly to the church by laying it at "the feet of the apostles," (Acts 4:34-35, 37; 5:2) the leaders of the church. Paul commanded Christians to give regularly to the leaders in their local church congregation (2 Cor 8-9; 1 Tim 5:17-18).

A fourth reason God allows us to make money is to actually enjoy it! This is true whether you make a lot of money or just a little money. Paul reminds rich Christians to keep the right balance with money: don't depend on your great wealth in place of God; but also remember that God allows you to make money for he "richly supplies us with all things to enjoy" (1 Tim 6:17). Further, he says that God has blessed us with all good gifts in this life, including marriage and food "to be gratefully shared in by those who believe and know the truth. For everything created by God is good, and nothing is to be rejected if it is received with gratitude" (4:3-4). Solomon reminded believers of God's benevolent intents for us while we are on the earth: "Here is what I have seen to be good and fitting: to eat, to drink, and enjoy oneself in all one's labor in which he labors under the sun *during* the few years of his life which God has given him; for this is his reward" (Eccl 5:18). The Psalmist rejoices that God "causes the grass to grow for the cattle, and vegetation for the labor of man, so that he may bring forth food from the earth, and wine which makes man's heart glad, so that he may make his face glisten with oil, and food which sustains man's heart" (Ps 104:14-15). God wants believers to enjoy life in a way that honors him as Creator, Savior and Judge. This enjoyment includes the wealth that God entrusts to our care.

Having established the theological foundation of what the Bible says about work and money, we are now in a position to look at some more practical elements related to retirement. In the next chapter, we will discuss the issue of retirement accounts.

5

STORING UP FOR THE FUTURE

Planning for the Future

This conversation about retirement naturally leads to a question of retirement accounts. You might be reading this book and thinking that our general argument leads to the conclusion that it is wrong for a Christian to save for retirement. Let us be clear: we are certainly *not* suggesting that you should give up saving for retirement. Firstly, such an argument would be inconsistent because both of us have a retirement plan with our church and are doing our best to plan responsibly for the future.

But secondly, we don't believe Scripture forbids saving for the future. Actually, biblical wisdom would compel us to make some effort at saving. Solomon, for example, contrasts the get-rich-quick scheme of the fool with the wise slow-growth-over-time approach of the wise man: "Wealth gained hastily will dwindle, but whoever gathers little by little will increase it." (Prov 13:11). Gathering little by little implies the intentional work of saving. We are also to follow the example of the ant who "gathers her food in harvest" (Prov 6:8), which is an act of saving (cf. Prov 10:5).

Saving for retirement is especially important for those in professions that require a significant amount of physical labor because there will come a day that such a person must retire and no longer be able to earn an income. Also, on average, we are living longer. The years that we are no longer able to earn an income but still require one are lengthening, making it necessary to save for retirement.[19]

Saving also enables us to meet our financial obligations. Paul instructs us to earn our living and become dependent upon no one (1 Thess 4:11-12). Of course, there may be times when our livelihood is wiped out—due to illness, natural disaster, some other devastating event—and we must become dependent upon someone else's financial kindness until we are back on our feet. But this possibility doesn't exempt us from wise planning and saving that guards us from

---

[19] For some practical help in planning financially for retirement, see C. J. Cagle, *Redeeming Retirement: A Practical Guide to Catch Up* (2021) and *Reimagine Retirement: Planning and Living for the Glory of God* (Nashville: B & H, 2019).

having to become financially dependent upon someone else.

Saving also allows us to be generous toward others. One of the joys of wise financial planning is having resources with which you can bless and provide for others who are in need. That believers would have some surplus to offer needy people is Paul's assumption when he writes, "Let the thief no longer steal, but rather let him labor, doing honest work with his own hands, so that he may have something to share with anyone in need" (Eph 4:28). We are to work, not only to provide for ourselves, but to also provide for those who are in need. Inevitably, such provision will flow from some amount of savings.

However, assuming that you will be able to afford to step away from work as you get older or no longer need regular income from a job, we want you to ask yourself these questions: How should I view my retirement? What am I saving *for*? What kind of lifestyle should I be aiming for in my latter years? If the Lord has blessed and you've been able to save and come to a point where you no longer need income from a job, what should you do with your life?

We want you to see that Scripture teaches us to plan well for the future, to trust God, and make it your aim to maintain fruitfulness as long as physically and mentally possible. Our goal with this book is to get you to think more biblically about your latter years, whether you are just starting your career or a few years from retirement or currently in retirement.

Perspective from Jesus

And, from the biblical texts we've already examined, we hope that you've started to see that your default hope shouldn't be to spend the last 15-20 years of your life in self-indulgent ease. So, how should I spend my retirement as a believer? To answer that question, we need to look at another biblical text that speaks directly to our modern conception of retirement. This passage contains an important story that Jesus told in response to a legal request from a crowd member.

> Someone in the crowd said to him, "Teacher, tell my brother to divide the inheritance with me." But he said to him, "Man, who made me a judge or arbitrator over you?" And he said to them, "Take care, and be on your guard against all covetousness, for one's life does not consist in the abundance of his possessions." And he told them a parable, saying, "The land of a rich man produced plentifully, and he thought to himself, 'What shall I do, for I have nowhere to store my crops?' And he said, 'I will do this: I will tear down my barns and build larger ones, and there I will store all my grain and my goods. And I will say to my soul, "Soul, you have ample goods laid up for many years; relax, eat, drink, be merry."' But God

said to him, 'Fool! This night your soul is required of you, and the things you have prepared, whose will they be?' So is the one who lays up treasure for himself and is not rich toward God" (Luke 12:13-21).

In response to the request for legal arbitration, Jesus responds with a word about covetousness. Apparently, the Lord sensed in this person's request an underlying greed and perhaps some unsavory motives for seeking his portion of the inheritance. Jesus follows his warning against covetousness with a story that resembles, in many ways, our present-day setting.

The land of a rich man "produced plentifully," which means that this man had enjoyed a highly productive and lucrative career. Because of his profitable working years, this man was able to put away a massive amount of financial provision—all his grain and goods—for his latter-years. Indeed, he had done so well that he needed larger barns to hold all that he had produced. In light of his massive wealth, he decided to retire: "And I will say to my soul, 'Soul, you have ample goods laid up for many years; relax, eat, drink, and be merry.'" But God's response to this attitude toward his wealth and life was in direct conflict with this man's expectations for retirement. "Fool! This night your soul is required of you, and the things you have prepared, whose will they be?'"

Here we have a man who had done very well in life. He had amassed great wealth over the last several years and had chosen to live off his wealth in relaxation and personal enjoyment for his remaining days. But it isn't even one day into his retirement that he dies and stands before God, having wasted his life. He was exceedingly rich with material goods, but he wasn't rich toward God. In other words, despite his financial success, he didn't know God in a saving relationship. His life, therefore, didn't reflect a God-centered, other-focused view of his wealth. Rather, he viewed his wealth as a means for his own luxury, comfort, and relaxation. The text makes it clear that God was not pleased with this man's self-centered, self-indulgent attitude toward his wealth and the idea of him spending his remaining years in self-serving ease.

Yet, this is precisely the way that many Americans—and, sadly, some professing Christians—view their own wealth and prospects for retirement. The goal for many is to stockpile enough cash and liquid assets to be able to stop working and spend the final ten to twenty years of their life in relative ease, pleasure-seeking, travel, and unencumbered relaxation.[20] If there were other biblical

---

[20] There are problems afoot, however. Some Americans are starting to realize they may not be able to afford retirement. See Noah Quint, "Too Many Americans Will Never be Able to Retire," at Bloomberg Quint, January 24, 2019. https://www.bloombergquint.com/view/america-needs-more-young-workers-to-support-aging-population. Accessed on January 28, 2022.

passages that better describe our American concept of retirement, you would be hard-pressed to find them.

Let us make the point clear: amassing wealth for the sake of future ease and a broad retreat from productive, other-oriented labor is a deplorable practice in God's sight. These kinds of expectations for our retiring years resist God's design and desire for his redeemed image bearers. As Christians, not only do we have insight from Scripture into our nature as human beings—fashioned by God to labor productively for our fellow man—we've also been born again (Titus 3:4-8). The image of God that sin previously defaced is now being renewed after the very image of its Creator (Col 3:10). So, not only do we have a clear picture of what God expects of his image-bearers, but we also have the spiritual resources from God to carry out this calling with diligence and joy. For the believer who grasps the biblical teaching on work, an early retirement characterized by aimless recreation and ease will be anathema. If we don't view such a lifestyle as undesirable, it is a sure sign that we've absorbed an American view of retirement rather than the biblical view.

Using Wealth Wisely

Even so, this story of the foolish rich man doesn't necessarily forbid saving for the future or saving for retirement. The problem wasn't the man's wealth as such. Scripture affirms that some Christians will be wealthy (1 Tim 6:17). The problem was the man's *use* of his wealth. His plan was to store up for a time of future ease and relaxation. God, however, does not entrust us with wealth so that we can only spend it on ourselves and secure a life of unproductive luxury. We are to steward our financial resources for the sake of furthering God's kingdom (Matt 25:14-31), to help those in need (Eph 4:28; Titus 3:14), and to support the church and other worthy gospel ministries (1 Cor 9:14; 16:1; 2 Cor 9:1-9). Given our current setting with concerns such as the cost of living, our employment, and our responsibility to care for those entrusted to our care, it is wise to save for a time when we won't be able to work the way we are currently working.

But even so, once we've come into retirement and have started to live off the wealth we've saved and the money we might be getting from the government in the form of a Social Security check, we are not to take this provision as a cue to step away from productive labor. Rather, we should see this as a time when we can pivot to a *new kind of labor*. We will talk about what this might look like in chapter 6. Here we only want to emphasize the biblical truth that God intends for us to keep engaging in productive labor as long as possible, even if we are able to stop working in a full-time, income-earning capacity.

Not all people will be able to retire in such a fashion. Some folks may have to continue working into their later years just to pay the bills. Others may need to move in with their adult children so that they might be cared for in their old age. When parents are unable to provide for themselves in their old age, God requires their children to honor their parents and provide for them financially (Exod 20:12; 1 Tim 5:4-8). This is not an excuse for parents to presume on their children, live irresponsibly and then saddle their adult children with extra financial responsibilities. But God's commandment at this point is clear: when parents are in need of financial provision, adult children are the ones who bear the responsibility to attend to their needs.

For those who are presently or will be able to retire without further need of a regular income, the question becomes, "How should I spend my retirement?" We will answer that question in the following chapter.

6

How to Spend Your Retirement Well

It's Not Too Late

If you are able to retire or must retire due to the nature of your work or your job's mandatory retirement policies, it will be necessary for you to determine *how* you will spend your retirement before you walk out of the office on your last day. If you are already retired but feel aimless in your day-to-day activities and lacking in a robust biblical vision for retirement, don't despair. You can still make important changes in your life to honor the Lord and make the best use of your retirement.

In his book, *Reimagine Retirement: Planning and Living for the Glory of God*, C. J. Cagle provides this biblically-grounded vision for life in our latter years: "A *reimagined retirement* is one that is planned, structured, lived, and continually reexamined in light of sound biblical doctrine, principles, and practice. It is a retirement lived for the glory of God, his kingdom, and his people."[21] We believe that Cagle gets the Christian view of retirement exactly right because it gets the Christian view of life right.

A Godward retirement that will honor Christ and bring satisfaction to our own souls is *planned*—Christian retirees should prepare actively for their retirement, not just financially, but with concrete ideas of how they will spend their last years for the benefit of others. It is *structured*—productive routines and spiritual disciplines remain in place and days are spent with intentionality. A retirement is actively *lived*, not passively accepted. But the overarching standard by which retirees are to shape their retirement years is the Word of God. That's why Christians must *continually reexamine* their retirement plans, aspirations, routines, and activities in light of *sound biblical doctrine, principles, and practice*. The motivation for such careful planning is not self, but *the glory of God, his kingdom, and his people.*

The common impulse when one considers retirement is to think first of the leisure and travel one can enjoy after working for a living. Now, we certainly aren't suggesting that there is anything wrong with spending some time in retirement traveling or engaging

---

[21] C. J. Cagle, *Reimagine Retirement: Planning and Living for the Glory of God* (Nashville: B & H, 2019), 44.

in restful, restorative, and refreshing recreation. Couples who have spent the last three decades working and raising children, for example, can rightfully look forward to a new season of time together, and this season may include some travel that previous obligations kept them from enjoying.

But let us also be just as clear: a Christian shouldn't make travel and leisure the aim of their life in retirement. In chapter 1 we noted that the impulse of the traditional retirees and the retire-early advocates was personal autonomy—freedom from the demands of an employer, or simply "self-rule." The Christian retiree, however, is never granted autonomy. Whether we are retired or gainfully employed, we are obliged to obey our heavenly Master, Jesus Christ, who is Lord (Rom 10:9). Even in our retirement we still bear the responsibility to steward our resources and opportunities for the glory of God. Jesus' parable of the talents extends to the *whole* of our lives, not just the years of peak energy and productivity. Let's consider this parable in a little detail.

Jesus the Master

In Matthew's Gospel (25:14-30), Jesus tells the story of a man who, prior to setting out on a journey, gathered his three servants and entrusted each of them with a portion of his property. To one of the servants, he gave five talents. To another, two. And to another, one talent. A talent in Jesus' day was a significant sum of money, so Jesus is making it clear that, while some were given more than others, each of these servants was each entrusted with a sizable allocation of their master's property. The first two servants took their portion, did some business in the marketplace, and each made a one-hundred percent return on their investment. The one with five talents made five more, and the servant with two talents made two more. The third servant, however, did not engage in any kind of business with his master's money. Rather, he hid the talent in the ground and failed to make any use of the property with which he was entrusted.

When the master returns, he takes an assessment of each servant's stewardship. Having doubled his master's money, the first servant reported with ten talents. The servant with two also doubled his master's property and now presented four talents. It's important to notice that the master didn't require any more from the servants than what he had given them. In other words, the master was pleased with the servant who produced the four talents because he had stewarded well what had been initially entrusted to him. There was no comparison of the final amounts between the first and second servant. What pleased the master is the multiplication of the amount they had originally received.

Things did not go as well for the third servant. This servant didn't offer any return on his master's property; he only produced the amount his master had originally given him. Feigning fear of his master's unreasonableness, the servant claimed that he was afraid and therefore hid his talent in the ground. He didn't gain anything, but neither did he lose anything. The master, however, immediately detected his servant's insincerity and pointed out his faulty logic. Had he really been afraid of the master's so-called unfairness, he would have deposited his talent in the bank—an otherwise safe place to park his money—and let it gather some interest while the master was gone. No, the deepest issue wasn't fear; it was laziness.

The characters and elements of the story and what they represent should be clear. Jesus is the master. His servants are those who claim to know and follow him. The talents represent everything that Christ has entrusted to us. This stewardship includes more than just our financial resources. The "talents" include everything that Christ has given us: wealth, non-liquid assets, personal skills, time, energy, health, spiritual gifts, opportunities, jobs, family, friends, and so on. We are responsible to steward *all* of these tangible and intangible items for the glory of God and the growth of the kingdom.[22]

---

[22] To view the talents as a mere reference to money or other financial assets is a failure to make the appropriate connection between the elements of the parable and their corresponding spiritual realities. In the parable, the master entrusts to his servants some of his property in the form of talents. This property would have included everything the master owned. As King

Obeying the Master

We are not given the option of whether to engage in careful, fruitful stewardship of Christ's property. We are commanded to comply! That's why Jesus ends the parable by underscoring the eternal state of the lazy servant: "And cast the worthless servant into the outer darkness. In that place there will be weeping and gnashing of teeth" (Matt 25:30). The servant who fails to multiply his master's property demonstrates that he doesn't really know the master. Jesus is not teaching that we are saved *by* our multiplication of his property. We are saved by grace alone through faith alone in Christ alone (Rom 4:5; Eph 2:8-9). But a servant who is saved by grace and knows this gracious Master will be a servant who stewards his Master's property well. He will be a servant who, energized by the Holy Spirit, is zealous for good works (Titus 2:14).

As we see in this parable, to presume that our retirement is a time in which we can unyoke ourselves from this stewardship is a spiritually dangerous venture. While retirement will likely be a time when the intensity of our labors is decreased, it cannot be a time when our labors cease altogether. With these biblical foundations

---

of the universe, Jesus owns everything (Acts 10:36; Rom 10:12). The property from which Jesus distributes each servant's allotment, therefore, is the whole world. The "talents" thus represent everything a person might possess, whether those possessions are tangible (money, property, goods, people), or intangible (spiritual gifts, energy, opportunities). The faithful steward is the one who uses all of these resources for their Godward end.

in place, let's consider practically how you might make the most of your retirement.

7

Do Not Grow Weary in Doing Good

Don't be Deceived

Let's now move on to other practical matters that can become challenges that come with getting older. To this end, a word from the apostle Paul will prove helpful. In the following passage, we find Paul's answer to our temptation to view our latter years as a time of taking a break from life:

> Do not be deceived: God is not mocked, for whatever one sows, that will he also reap. For the one who sows to his own flesh will from the flesh reap corruption, but the one who sows to the Spirit will from the Spirit reap

eternal life. And let us not grow weary of doing good, for in due season we will reap, if we do not give up. So then, as we have opportunity, let us do good to everyone, and especially to those who are of the household of faith (Gal 6:7-10).

Paul starts this passage by warning the Galatians to not be deceived. Deceived about what? Deceived about the way reality works. God has built into this world the principle of sowing and reaping. What you sow, you will certainly reap. That's a guarantee. God will not be mocked.

The question is what will you reap? Well, if you sow your *flesh*, you will reap *corruption*. If you sow to the Spirit, you will reap eternal life. What does this mean? It means that if your life is characterized by sowing to the flesh, you need to be deeply concerned about whether you are a genuine Christian, because a life characterized by sowing to the flesh will end in corruption which is the opposite, in this text, of eternal life. Corruption here is eternal judgment.[23] Therefore, Paul encourages the

---

[23] Thomas Schreiner explains, "…the contrast indicates that corruption refers to final destruction and final judgment, whereas those who sow to the Spirit 'will reap eternal life'….Since 'eternal life' is contrasted with 'corruption,' the latter means that one will not enjoy the life of the coming age, while the former refers to the eschatological reward of life that is promised to those who sow to the Spirit. Paul's gospel of grace in Galatians does not countenance moral laxity" (*Galatians,* Exegetical Commentary on the New Testament [Grand Rapids: Zondervan, 2010], 369). John Brown,

Galatians to press on and not grow weary in doing good because such persons will eventually reap eternal life if they don't give up. Practically, this means: "as we have opportunity, let us do good to everyone, and especially to those who are of the household of faith."

We chose this text in this discussion on retirement for three reasons. First, what else is a selfish, self-focused, recreation-filled retirement but a sowing to the flesh? A clear application of this warning, then, is to take care that we don't sow to the flesh in our latter years by pursuing a life of sheer ease, relaxation, and self-centered indulgence.

Don't Grow Weary

Second, Paul encourages us to not grow weary in doing good, which is a temptation that we might coddle during retirement. We could say, "I've worked hard, life's been tough, I finally have a chance for some rest and relaxation," and in so doing effectively "check out" of life for the next ten to twenty years. But Paul counters this temptation and tendency by saying, "Do not grow weary in doing good, for you will someday reap eternal life, *if you do not give up.*" Paul is not suggesting that genuine Christians can lose their salvation, or that their

---

commenting on Galatians over 170 years ago, says it well: "No man who is habitually neglectful of, or allowedly languid and careless in, the discharge of Christian duty, can have satisfactory evidence of being an object of Divine favour; and if, in these circumstances, he cherishes a confidence in the goodness of his state, and in the security of his salvation, his confidence is presumptuous." (*Galatians*, Geneva Series of Commentaries [Carlisle, PA: Banner of Truth, 2001; repr., 1853], 346).

right standing with God is dependent upon their works (see Gal 2:16). But Paul knows that true believers don't retreat into self-serving ease, so he offers a sharp warning to remind us what will happen if we do: we won't inherit eternal life. Such a warning is not meant to undermine our assurance, but instead to deepen and strengthen it as we heed the warning and keep doing good.

Third, Paul gets practical and tells us what our retirement years *should* look like: "as we have opportunity, let us do good to everyone, and especially to those who are of the household of faith." (Gal 6:9) Doing good to everyone, especially other believers, is what should characterize a Christian's lifestyle, even in his or her retirement years (see also 1 Thess 5:15). This means that one of the features of your retirement that you should look forward to most is the opportunity to serve in greater capacities at your local church. Sadly, some Christian retirees are spending so much time on vacations and visiting family that their attendance at their local congregation becomes inconsistent and unreliable.

This is a sad situation because one's latter years are precisely the season that older Christians should be using their extra time to disciple the next generation. Scripture expects and instructs the older men and women to pour into the younger men and women in their church. Older, more seasoned saints are vital to the spiritual health and equilibrium of the Body of

Christ. Every local church needs the reservoir of experience, wisdom, and steadiness that only the mature can provide. God puts a premium on the value of saints who have walked the long road of life being faithful to Him. God says of older believers, "a gray head is a crown of glory" (Prov 16:31) and "The glory of young men is their strength, and the honor of old men is their gray hair" (Prov 20:29). The zeal, enthusiasm and stamina that young people can bring to a congregation is needed and valuable, but there is no substitute for the balance of wisdom, realism and a long-term perspective that is added to the local church by its seniors.

As pastors, we are disheartened that, at many churches we know of, there is no stabilizing base of senior saints in their congregations to speak of. Such a congregation, lacking sufficient influence from its senior saints, is out of kilter and vulnerable to deception, rash decisions, and pride that young people are especially prone to (cf. 1 Tim 3:6). There is no better illustration of this all-too-often occurrence than in the days just after Solomon died when his prideful son, Rehoboam, assumed the throne. The citizens of Israel came to the new young king and petitioned him to lighten the burdens that Solomon his father had foisted on the people. Before deciding what to do, Rehoboam asked for three days to get counsel. He sought counsel from the experienced elders, and then he asked the opinion of his younger friends. Tragically, Rehoboam did not value the older, wiser saints in his community.

The tragic, infamous account reads as follows:

> And King Rehoboam consulted with the elders who had served his father Solomon while he was still alive, saying, "How do you advise *me* to answer this people?" Then they spoke to him, saying, "If you will be a servant to this people today, and will serve them and grant them their request, and speak pleasant words to them, then they will be your servants always." But he ignored the advice of the elders which they had given him, and consulted with the young men who had grown up with him and served him. He said to them, "What advice do you give, so that we may answer this people who have spoken to me, saying, 'Lighten the yoke which your father put on us'?" And the young men who had grown up with him spoke to him, saying, "This is what you should say to this people who spoke to you, saying: 'Your father made our yoke heavy, now you make it lighter for us!' You should speak this way to them: 'My little finger is thicker than my father's waist! Now then, my father loaded you with a heavy yoke; yet I will add to your yoke. My father disciplined you with whips, but I will discipline you with scorpions!'" (1 Kings 12:6-11).

The local church needs the ongoing, stabilizing, influence of its retirees. Younger Christians need their help on how to navigate this troubled life with its many unexpected challenges. Seniors have already blazed a trail in life that the next generation needs to follow. Older saints need to show younger believers the way on a practical level. Paul put it this way: "Older men are to be temperate, dignified, self-controlled, sound in faith, in love, in perseverance. Older women likewise *are to be* reverent in their behavior, not malicious gossips nor enslaved to much wine, teaching what is good, so that they may encourage the young women to love their husbands, to love their children, *to be* sensible, pure, workers at home, kind, being subject to their own husbands, so that the word of God will not be dishonored" (Titus 2:2-5). John also showcases the unique contribution senior saints make to the local congregation when he said, "I am writing to you, fathers, because you know Him who has been from the beginning" (1 John 2:13). In this context, "fathers" refers to older people in the congregation, and John is commending them for their deeply-rooted faith and sure walk with God that results from a long life well lived.

Too often, however, Christian young men and women looking for godly discipleship are disappointed to find that the older saints are rarely around enough to develop deep relationships or to offer the wisdom they've stored up over a lifetime of knowing God.

Indeed, if the retirees are not regularly in the church, the young men and women in fact will be hindered in their spiritual growth, for it is only those who walk *with* the wise who become wise (Prov 13:20). By planning your retirement years to be lived *away* from your local church, you undermine God's plan for discipleship and hurt the coming generation of saints.

Recalibrate

Practically, this may mean—contrary to how many manage their retirement today—that you travel less, or you choose to live in one location rather than traversing between a winter and summer home six-months out of the year. Granted, this practice of remaining well-rooted in your local church and resisting the allure of multi-week jaunts through Europe or summering in Santa Barbara will likely appear out-of-step with what your unbelieving neighbors are doing. But our Lord calls older men and women to train the younger generation, and this training can only be effectively facilitated by older saints who are consistently available and accessible.

As it turns out, not only is following Paul's instruction in Titus 2:1-5 an important part of Christian obedience for older saints, but such obedience in serving the younger men and women in one's local church will bring older saints more satisfaction than will constant travel, pleasure-seeking, and summer homes. Paul's greatest delight on this earth was centered in the people to whom he had the privilege of ministering (Phil 4:1; 1 Thess 2:19; 2 Thess 1:4). The joy of pouring one's life and God-given wisdom into younger believers, beholding their growth in Christ, and experiencing deep, gospel-grounded relationships are the greatest delights we can experience in this life (see also Ps 16:3). Paul did not derive his satisfaction from a catalog full of exotic travel excursions or recreational pursuits; he found his greatest pleasure in the names and faces of the people that he served and blessed through his gospel-centered counsel (e.g., Rom 16:1-16). We will also find the same satisfaction as we resist the American dream of a leisurely retirement and embrace a greater joy of a retirement spent for the good of our fellow believers, particularly those of the younger generation.

Again, however, the exhortation to not grow weary in doing good is not just a nudge to choose a lifestyle that provides you with more personal fulfillment. Paul's statements in Galatians 6:7-10 are a warning to not allow the temptations that attend older age and retirement to derail us from persevering in the faith. Christians who are in their retirement years face a slew of new temptations that they did not likely experience—at least not to the same degree—when they were younger. Illness, weakness, weariness, boredom, and the cultural pull to structure one's retirement around personal interests and hobbies will all conspire to pull you away from a life of active good works for the glory of God. Older believers must be aware of these temptations that tend to be unique to folks in their retirement years.

Personal illness and physical weakness, for example, may tempt us to excuse ourselves from serving the body of Christ. While illness and weakness may limit or even halt our ministry for a season, we cannot allow these troubles to keep us from serving others or to conclude that we have nothing to offer. This is where understanding the biblical teaching on spiritual gifts is helpful. When we were saved, God gave us a spiritual gift or set of gifts that He will never remove from us in this life (Rom 12:6). Therefore, even when we are older and weaker, we still possess spiritual gifts, and these gifts are what God intends for us to use to bless the body of Christ (1 Cor 12:7). No matter our age, we are vital to the church's health and growth (1 Cor 12:14-26).

Older folks are also more susceptible to the ensnarement of too much television watching. One study showed that adults aged sixty-five and older watch three times as much television as do younger adults.[24] The study concluded, further, that even as older adults watch appreciably more television than younger adults, on the whole these older adults liked television *less* than did their younger counterparts. The study also found that such a high amount of television consumption was

---

[24] Colin A. Depp, Ph.D., David A. Schkade, Ph.D., Wesley K. Thompson, Ph.D., and Dilip V. Jeste, M.D., "Age, Affective Experience, and Television Use," in *The American Journal of Preventative Medicine* 39.2 (Aug 2010): 173-78.

connected to greater health problems due to the sedentary nature of the television-watching experience.

The researchers also isolated a few reasons that could account for such an excess of television watching among older people as compared to younger people. One factor, of course, is increased free time. Another is the fact that barriers to recreational activities increase as one gets older. Unlike traveling, exercise, reading, outdoor recreation and community activities, television watching has little to no obstacles to overcome before one can partake in it, nor is much effort required to engage in the activity.

While we aren't making a case for eliminating television viewing altogether, we do want to highlight, in light of the biblical based wisdom and principles put forth earlier, the temptation for retirees to watch too much of it. As the above study observed, there are factors that are unique to retirement that can more easily ensnare older people. The ease with which someone can fritter their day away by watching television makes this temptation especially acute. Christians, therefore, need to be aware of this temptation and, by grace, fight against it. Why is this necessary? Because the television can be a means to sowing to the flesh in your latter years. Rather than spending your time in fruitful, other-oriented service, the spiritual disciplines and other edifying activities, you face the danger of becoming entranced by, and over-invested in, a form of entertainment that has diminishing returns, wastes one's valuable and non-recapturable time, and infiltrates the mind and heart with content that is designed to stir up sinful inclinations.

Caring for the Homebound

The church also needs to come alongside elderly folks who may be significantly homebound and help them make the most of their time. While older saints are responsible to disciple the younger generation, the church as a whole should take deliberate interest in ministering to retirees. One particular group of retirees that needs help honoring Christ in their later years are the homebound. Related to what we just noted about television watching, saints who are homebound may find it especially challenging to make the most of their waking hours for Christ. Television becomes an easy way to pass the hours, and thus can become the primary activity for elderly men and women who are essentially confined to their homes throughout the week. An important ministry for younger believers is not only to visit these dear saints, talk with them, and provide them a little company, but also to actively assist these homebound saints in managing their daily routines in a way that honors Christ.

Also necessary is a similar kind of ministry to older saints who are presently in an elderly care facility. Too often in these facilities, older men and women are left to pass their days in front of a common television or with amusements that do little to edify their souls.

Younger believers should visit these saints, read the Bible to them, and pray with them. But they should also, in accordance with the older saint's abilities (some elderly folks in care facilities being largely incapacitated), help them to develop a daily routine that builds their souls and blesses those around them.

8

TRUE RETIREMENT

Worldview Clash

This entire book can be summed up as a portrait of a clash between two worldviews: what the secular world says the goal of this life is versus what the Bible says the goal is. The world says, "Live for today! Live for self! Focus on the here and now!"—in other words, live like the rich fool Jesus mentioned, whose *mantra* for life was, "take your ease, eat, drink and be merry" (Luke 12:19). And similarly, like the pragmatic hedonist that Paul mocked, whose motto was, "Let us eat and drink, for tomorrow we die" (1 Cor 15:32).

In contrast, the Bible says that life is more than this present, short, and fading physical life. God puts a premium on the spiritual life and the eternal. That is what sets the Christian worldview apart from the typical, myopic and short-sighted counterpart exalted in secular American culture. Christians are called by God to live in light of the future; in light of an imminent death after which we will then face judgment; in light of Christ's return to earth in power and glory; and in light of life in the next world that will last forever. This present world is not our home, "For our citizenship is in heaven, from which also we eagerly wait for a Savior, the Lord Jesus Christ, who will transform the body of our humble state into conformity with the body of His glory, by the exertion of the power that He has even to subject all things to Himself" (Phil 3:20-21).

Be Ready

Jesus commanded his followers to be ready for his return and to live in constant anticipation of his Second Coming. He said, "Be on the alert then, for you do not know the day nor the hour" (Matt 25:13). Paul's motive for living today was based upon the reality of facing Christ tomorrow. This should be the underlying motive for every Christian: "it is appointed for men to die once and after this comes judgment" (Heb 9:27). Like Paul we are to hold "fast the word of life, so that in the day of Christ I will have reason to glory because I did not run in vain nor toil in vain" (Phil 2:16). To "run in vain" is to live life in an aimless, idle, self-serving manner, ignoring Christ as the priority. To "toil in vain" is to work, labor, and invest in the wrong priorities with the wrong ultimate goal in mind. This applies to retirement. The goal in this life, as framed in the Bible for the Christian, is not to retire and thereafter detach and pursue a life of ease and earthly bliss. The Christian's goal in this life is to always be living in a way that pleases Christ and advances His kingdom, even though what that looks like will change with the seasons of one's life. For the God-honoring, Christ-exalting, Spirit-filled, obedient child of God, "Eat, drink and be merry" needs to be replaced with "Whether, then, you eat or drink or whatever you do, do all to the glory of God" (1 Cor 10:31). And in order to do all things to the glory of God, we need to make sure we have the right overall view of the meaning of life. We need to see the big picture; the ultimate long-term picture. And that picture is eternity as God has revealed it. As Paul reminds us again, "keep seeking the things above, where Christ is, seated at the right hand of God. Set your mind on the things above, not on the things that are on earth" (Col 3:1-2). A key phrase here that informs our view of retirement is, "keep seeking the things above." Christians are to "keep seeking" heavenly things even after they hit the ages of fifty-five, or sixty-two, or sixty-five, or any other senior-denominated age.

The fact is, for the believer, there is no real "retirement" in this life. We don't retire from seeking to please God with all our might in every area of life (Rom 12:1-2). The depiction the Bible gives is that there is no real "rest" in this life. There is only real, true, fulfilling rest in the next life, in heaven, with Christ, the Father and the Spirit. John the Apostle put it this way:

> Here is the perseverance of the saints who keep the commandments of God and their faith in Jesus. And I heard a voice from heaven, saying, "Write: 'Blessed are the dead who die in the Lord from now on!'" "Yes," says the Spirit, "so that they may rest from their labors, for their deeds follow with them" (Rev 14:12-13).

When we die is when we truly rest from our labors and are welcomed into paradise with Christ (Luke 23:43; Phil 1:12; Rev 6:11). In the meantime, until we die, we need to serve God proactively, in keeping with whatever abilities we possess during the latter stages of our lives. Think of Anna in Luke 2 at the time of Christ's birth. She was in her eighties (and maybe even older than that), yet she was active, with the saints daily, serving in God-focused ministry. She did not, as the cliché goes, "hang up the towel" and retreat into isolation in the proverbial rocking chair away from God's people. God was pleased with her proactive approach to life in her "retirement" years. And to boot, she was a widow. Anna was an exemplary model of selfless, life-long service to Christ. What motivated her rigorous, seasoned, octogenarian service to God? The motivation was living in light of the future, in light of what Scripture said about the next life and eternity (Luke 2:38).

One way that can revolutionize the way you think about retirement as you strive to live in light of the future is by regularly meditating on the doctrine of eternal rewards. God will reward his people in the next life based on how they live in this life and such rewards are a healthy motivation for how we live now. One of the last things Jesus ever said was, "Behold, I am coming quickly, and My reward is with Me, to render to every man according to what he has done" (Rev 22:12). Paul did not retire from life or Christian service in old age. He kept serving until every last drop of his blood was spilled out. And he kept living for Christ aggressively until death because he was motivated by eternal rewards:

> For I am already being poured out as a drink offering, and the time of my departure has come. I have fought the good fight, I have finished the course, I have kept the faith; in the future there is reserved for me the crown of righteousness, which the Lord, the righteous Judge, will award to me on that day; and not only to me, but also to all who have loved His appearing" (2 Tim 4:6-8).

In light of this important truth, let's highlight some key points of eternal heavenly rewards.

God Will Judge Every Person
No one will escape God's judgment in the next life.

Every soul belongs to God (Ezek 18:4). When Christ returns at the end of the age while a person is then living, or when a person dies before that time, God the Creator "will render to each person according to his deeds" (Rom 2:6; cf. Ps 62:12). A day of ultimate accounting is coming. God declared, "Vengeance is Mine, I will repay" (Rom 12:19). Christ will return in a fury of glory "to judge the living and the dead, and by His appearing and His kingdom" (2 Tim 4:1). At the time of judgment everything will be revealed. God will expose every human secret. There is no place to hide: "For God will bring every act to judgment, everything which is hidden, whether it is good or evil" (Eccl 12:14). "And there is no creature hidden from His sight, but all things are open and laid bare to the eyes of Him with whom we have to do" (Heb 4:13).

Rewards are Based on Our Works

Salvation and forgiveness of sin are not attained by human works, but our rewards are. Heavenly rewards are based on acts of obedience and faithfulness to God's commands. Unbelievers cannot obey God in a way that pleases Him (Heb 11:6), and therefore he or she will not receive heavenly rewards. Unbelievers will only incur condemnation, punishment and pain (Rom 2:5-6; Rev 14:9-11). Believers will receive heavenly rewards which will be in proportion to their faithfulness in this life. We saw this earlier in the parable of the talents (Matt 25:14-30). Paul put it this way: "For we must all appear before the judgment seat of Christ, so that each one may receive compensation for his deeds *done* through the body, in accordance with what he has done, whether good or bad" (2 Cor 5:10). Furthermore, Paul says, "For no one can lay a foundation other than the one which is laid, which is Jesus Christ. Now if anyone builds on the foundation with gold, silver, precious stones, wood, hay, *or* straw, each one's work will become evident; for the day will show it because it is *to be* revealed with fire, and the fire itself will test the quality of each one's work. If anyone's work which he has built on it remains, he will receive a reward" (1 Cor 3:11-14).

There are Degrees of Rewards

Some of the heavenly rewards God blesses believers with will be the same, such as citizenship in heaven, access to God's presence, a resurrection body, sinless human status, and more. But there will also be personalized rewards that are different from one person to the next. And many of these differences in rewards are based on varying degrees of faithfulness of service with which one operates in this life. Some saints will receive more rewards than others. Not everyone will be totally equal in ability, function, and ownership in heaven. "From each according to his ability, to each according to his needs" will not be a principle in God's city. No Marxism in the Millennium Kingdom or the New Jerusalem! Rather the principle will be, "From God's sovereign discretion, to each according to his faithfulness." Regarding a person who is faithful in this life with a "few" things, Jesus says He will put that person in charge of "many" things in the next life (Matt 25:21). In Luke 19, Jesus gave one servant charge over ten cities while He gave the other servant charge over five cities. He rewarded each servant with a different degree of responsibility, yet each reward was intended and received as a blessing. In contrast, some Christians' work will be exposed as worthless wood, hay and stubble when God burns it away into nothingness at the judgment seat of Christ. Only investments in true spiritual realities during this life, ventures that Paul describes as "gold, silver and precious stones," will be rewarded. Living for retirement ease and pleasure-seeking will yield wood, hay, and stubble; living every single day of our allotted time in the light of Christ's upcoming return and subsequent eternal reign will produce a yield equivalent to gold, silver, and precious stones.

You Can Squelch Your Rewards

It is possible for a Christian to sabotage his or her own future evaluation before the heavenly throne of Christ on judgment day by slipping into laziness, disobedience, loss of focus—in other words, by becoming self-oriented or by giving up prior to properly finishing the race that is called the Christian life. We need to run the Christian race through the finish line. And our goal is not just to finish the race, for Paul says we are to live the Christian life with the aim of "winning" the way an Olympic athlete presses on for victory (1 Cor 9:24). So don't just run the race; run it to win. Having a wrong view of retirement can undermine your own Christian race. We saw in the previous chapter that as we get older, there are unique temptations that will seek to lure us away from faithfulness to productive ministry for Christ. Jesus warned believers about losing focus: "Hold firmly to what you have, so that no one will take your crown" (Rev 3:11).

We all need to heed the above biblical reminders. God requires us to live life in view of the big picture, his ultimate plan, focusing our energies on spiritual, heavenly and eternal truths. The prospect of someday facing Jesus as our Judge and being rewarded by Him with greater heavenly rewards, is a major healthy incentive for staying true to God's priorities while avoiding the strong pull in the direction of a worldview that is ever calling, "Live it up now, while you can! It's all about you!" We know better. The authentic Christian life is all about pleasing the Father and living for Christ (2 Cor 5:9). The biblical and Christian worldview is radically different from that of the world with respect to retirement. Our goal is to live each day as a living sacrifice for Him until He welcomes us into His kingdom of rest.

9

Conclusion

The Bible is sufficient for meeting all our needs and answering all our questions about how to live life in a way that pleases God. Through our relationship with Christ came by believing the gospel, God's "divine power has granted to us everything pertaining to life and godliness" (2 Pet 1:3). Such sufficiency applies to our understanding of retirement and our plans for our twilight years.

In chapter one we looked at the typical definition of retirement and the purpose of this life, which sadly is frequently at odds with God's Word. The world emphasizes immediate short-term gratification, prioritizing temporal life instead of spiritual and eternal life. In chapter two we explained how America acquired

Conclusion

such a myopic, crass, and self-centered view of retirement. In chapter three we looked to the Bible to establish a theology of work. God created humans to be productive, labor hard, produce wealth to sustain a living and share with others. Chapter four provided a theology-based explanation of money and wealth. God created wealth, He's sovereign over it, we are to be faithful stewards of what He entrusts to our care, and investing in His Church, His ministries and His kingdom in all forms of Christian service are to be life-long pursuits and priorities of every Christian. Chapter five gave Jesus' perspective from Luke 12 on how we should view the future, and especially on how we can plan for the end of life in a way that pleases Christ. Chapter six talked more specifically about how to be good stewards in our later years based on Jesus' wisdom imparted in Matthew 25. In chapter seven we were reminded from the sixth chapter of Galatians that God requires all believers to never grow weary of doing good. Older saints may transition out of previous labors, but their later years are to be a season to bless the Body of Christ in new ways with their God-given wisdom that they have gained over time. We closed out the book with chapter eight, with a summary of the biblical theology of eternal rewards, which is one of the heavenly motives for service, work and goal-setting in this life. As the Bible teaches, true retirement and rest come in the next life, in heaven, as a reward from God. This life is to be about serving Him.

Earthly life is a gift, but it is a gift that God calls us to steward well for His glory. The weaknesses and illnesses that come with old age, coupled with a cultural view of retirement that sees our latter years as a season of unfettered ease, can collude to derail even the most well-intentioned Christian. Instead of spending the last few years of life for the glory of God and the good of our church and neighbor, we are tempted to focus on personal fulfillment, interests, and the general comforts that comes with retirement. Our prayer is that the biblical truth included in this little book will help you set a course (or reset your current course) toward a Christ-exalting retirement. It will not likely look the same as your neighbor's retirement. You may not enjoy as many vacations or time spent on the golf course as the folks in the house across the street. But you will someday hear your Savior say, "Well done, good and faithful servant," and that's infinitely better than a few years of adult playtime.

For those interested in more study on this topic and related issues from a biblical perspective, we recommend the following resources:

- Randy Alcorn, *Money, Possessions and Eternity*, Wheaton: Tyndale House, 1989

- Ron Blue, Larry Burkett, and Jeremy White, *The Burkett and Blue to Securing Wealth to Last: Money Essentials for the Second Half of Life*, Nashville: B & H, 2003

Conclusion

- Ron Blue, *Master Your Money*, Nashville: Thomas Nelson, 1986

- C. J. Cagle *Reimagine Retirement: Planning and Living for the Glory of God*, Nashville: B & H, 2019

- C. J. Cagle, *Redeeming Retirement: A Practical Guide to Catch Up*, n.p., 2021

- John MacArthur, *Whose Money Is It Anyway? A Biblical Guide to God's Wealth*, Nashville: Thomas Nelson, 2000

ABOUT THE AUTHORS

Originally from Montana, Derek Brown received his undergraduate degree from The Master's University (Santa Clarita, CA) and his M.Div. and Ph.D. from Southern Baptist Theological Seminary (Louisville, KY). He serves as an associate pastor at Creekside Bible Church in Cupertino, California and Academic Dean of the Cornerstone Bible College and Seminary. He is the author of *Strong and Courageous: The Character and Calling of Mature Manhood*, *How to Pray for Your Pastor*, and *Solomon's Great Commission*. Derek lives with his wife and three children in the San Francisco Bay Area.

Cliff McManis is an elder and the teaching-pastor at Creekside Bible Church in Cupertino, CA. He graduated from The Master's University and The Master's Seminary. In addition to shepherding in the local church, he also serves as Associate Professor of Theology training pastors at The Cornerstone Bible College and Seminary in Vallejo, CA. He is the author of several books, including *Apologetics by the Book*, *The Biblically-Driven Church* and *What the Bible Says about Confrontation*. He serves as the General Editor of With All Wisdom Publications. Cliff and his family live in Northern California.

ABOUT WITH ALL WISDOM

With All Wisdom is the Christian media creation ministry located in Cupertino, CA. We started this publishing ministry out of the simple desire to serve the local body with substantive biblical resources for the sake of our people's growth and spiritual maturity.

But we also believe that book publishing, like any other Christian ministry, should first and foremost be under the supervision and accountability of the local church. While we are grateful for and will continue to support the many excellent traditional publishers available today—our shelves are full of the books they have produced—we also believe that the best place to develop solid, life-giving theology and biblical instruction is within the local church.

With All Wisdom is also unique because we offer print versions of our books at a very low cost while making all of our books digitally accessible for free at WithAllWisdom.org. We strive for excellence in our writing and seek to provide a high-quality product to our readers. Our editorial team is comprised of men and women who are highly trained and excellent in their craft. But since we are able to avoid the high overhead costs that are typically incurred by traditional publishers, we are able to pass significant savings on to you. The result is a growing collection of books that are substantive, readable, and affordable.

In order to best serve various spiritual and theological needs of the body of Christ, we have developed three distinct lines of books. **Big Truth | little books**® provides readers with accessible, manageable works on theology, Christian living, and important church and social issues in a format that is easy to read and easy to finish. Our **Equip Series** is aimed at Christians who desire to delve a little deeper into doctrine and practical matters of the faith. Our **Foundations Series** is our academic line in which we seek to contribute to the contemporary theological discussion by combining pastoral perspective with rigorous scholarship.

OTHER TITLES FROM WITH ALL WISDOM PUBLICATIONS

Please visit us at WithAllWisdom.org
to learn more about these titles

BIG TRUTH little books®

A Biblical View of Trials
Cliff McManis

What the Bible Says About Gray Areas
Cliff McManis

Faith: The Gift of God
Cliff McManis

The Problem of Evil
Cliff McManis

What the Bible Says About Government
Cliff McManis

God Defines and Defends Marriage
Cliff McManis

How to Pray for Your Pastor
Derek Brown

Protecting the Flock: The Priority of Church Membership
Cliff McManis

Educating Your Child: Public, Private, or Homeschool? A Biblical Perspective
Cliff McManis

What the Bible Says About Depression
Cliff McManis

What the Bible Says About Confrontation
Cliff McManis

Fellowship with God:
A Guide to Bible Reading, Meditation, and Prayer
Derek Brown

What the Bible Says About Hospitality
Cliff McManis

The Danger of Hypocrisy:
Coming to Grips with Jesus' Most Damning Sermon
J.R. Cuevas

*Solomon's Great Commission: A Theology of
Earthly Life*
Derek Brown

What the Bible Says About the Future
Colin Eakin

The Parable of Sports
J.R. Cuevas

Equip

*The Biblically-Driven Church:
How Jesus Builds His Body*
Cliff McManis

*God's Glorious Story:
The Truth of What It's All About*
Colin Eakin

*Strong and Courageous:
The Character and Calling of Mature Manhood*
Derek Brown

*The Gospel, the Church, and Homosexuality:
How the Gospel is Still the Power of God
for Redemption and Transformation*
Edited by Michael Sanelli and Derek Brown

Skillfully Surveying the Scriptures, Vol. 1: Genesis through Esther
J.R. Cuevas

Beware of Dogs: Exposing Error in the Modern Church
Colin Eakin

What the Bible Says About Israel: Past, Present & Future
Cliff McManis

Deacons: Clarifying the Biblical Role
J. Robert Douglas

Foundations

Apologetics by the Book
Cliff McManis

Made in the USA
Monee, IL
09 August 2023